T0112354

GET OFF YOUR iPHONE NOW!

Copyright © Summersdale Publishers Ltd, 2018, 2019.

First Published by Summersdale Publishers Ltd, an imprint of Hachette UK, 2018.

First Racehorse Publishing edition, 2019.

All Rights Reserved. No part of this book may be reproduced in any manner without the express written consent of the publisher, except in the case of brief excerpts in critical reviews or articles. All inquiries should be addressed to Racehorse Publishing, 307 West 36th Street, 11th Floor, New York, NY 10018.

Racehorse Publishing books may be purchased in bulk at special discounts for sales promotion, corporate gifts, fund-raising, or educational purposes. Special editions can also be created to specifications. For details, contact the Special Sales Department, Skyhorse Publishing, 307 West 36th Street, 11th Floor, New York, NY 10018 or info@skyhorsepublishing.com.

Racehorse Publishing™ is a pending trademark of Skyhorse Publishing, Inc.®, a Delaware corporation.

Visit our website at www.skyhorsepublishing.com.

10 9 8 7 6 5 4 3 2

Library of Congress Cataloging-in-Publication Data is available on file.

Text by Emily Kearns
Cover image by Getty Images

ISBN: 978-1-63158-368-1
E-Book ISBN: 978-1-63158-369-8

Printed in the United States of America

GET OFF YOUR iPHONE NOW!

FASCINATING TRIVIA, AMAZING FACTS, AND FUN ACTIVITIES TO FREE YOU FROM YOUR SCREEN

KATE FREEMAN

RACEHORSE PUBLISHING

CONTENTS

Introduction 7

Nature 8

Attract butterflies into your garden 9

Figure out when the sun is going to set 10

Teach a parrot to talk 11

Build a bird feeder 12

Make a natural bird feeder 14

Watch a meteor shower 15

Hold a chicken 16

Gauge the proximity of a storm 17

Outrun a crocodile 18

Know your crocodiles from your alligators 19

Know your elephants 20

Learn animal family names 21

Know your collective creature names 22

Science 23

Get power from a potato 24

Measure humidity 26

Grow crystals 27

Stick a balloon to the wall 28

Learn the first 30 elements 29

Play glow-in-the-dark bowling 30

Wow your friends with space facts 31

Know your bones 32

Make jelly set quickly 34

Create giant bubbles 35

Make a homemade volcano 36

History 37

Memorize the English monarchs 38

Brush up on your US presidents 40

Know your twentieth- and twenty-first-century UK prime ministers 42

Learn about the major conflicts since 1899 that involved the US 44

Remember important dates 45

Discover influential US politicians and activists 46

Learn about top inventors 47

Learn the capitals of European countries 48

Geography 50

Know the top 10 largest countries by area 51

Learn the Countries of Central and South America 52

Learn all 50 US states 54

Work your head around population density 55
Name all of the Hawaiian islands 56
Know the counties of England 57
Learn about Antarctica 58
Measure the Earth 59
Know your continents 60
Learn the countries of Africa 61
Know your bodies of water 62
Into the Deep 63

Words and Language 64
Try cockney rhyming slang 65
World languages 66
Write flash fiction 67
Compose a haiku 68
Send a postcard 69
Learn Roman numerals 70
Speak Pig Latin 71
Learn Morse code 72
Famous Messages 74
Most common languages spoken in homes in the US 75
Create your own language 76
Know your British English 77
Learn semaphore 78
Keep the art of letter writing alive 80

Food 81
Pickle onions 82
Know your plant food families 83
Grow your name 84
Master chopsticks 85
Make chocolate fridge cake 86
Make cookies last longer 87
Roast sweet chestnuts 88
Crack a coconut 89
Keep flies out of your kitchen 90
Dry chilies 91
How to make your drink cold quickly 92
Make an egg stand up 93
Know your pastas and how to serve them 94
Make your own granola 96
Chop onions without crying 97

Sport and Fitness 98
Hold tree pose 99
Take your own pulse (or someone else's) 100
Learn the top ten most decorated Olympians 101
Build up to a 5k run 102
Know the top ten goalscorers Major League Soccer (MLS) 104
Eat a breakfast of champions 105

Meditate for ten minutes 106
Learn some new swimming strokes 108
Learn the top 100 m sprinters 110
Learn the top tennis Grand Slam winners 111
Know your FIFA World Cup winners 112
Step it up 113

The Arts 114
Learn the five most expensive works of art sold at auction 115
Make an origami bird 116
Draw a face 118
Master the nose flute 120
Learn to play the castanets 121
Change the color of a flower 122
Take a great photograph 123
Learn the top ten best-selling albums of all time 124
Know your discs 125
Create marbled paper 126
Know your recent Pulitzer Prize for Fiction winners 127
Learn the bestselling fiction books of all time 128

Etiquette 129
Wear flowers in your hair 130
Make decorative flags from old clothes 131
Tie a bow tie 132
Lay a table for a dinner party 134
Walk in heels 136
Learn about tipping practices 137
Wear a silk scarf 138
Dress for the occasion 140
Send thank-you notes 141
Make mocktails 142
Be the perfect host 144

Games 145
Turn right 146
Keep a poker face 147
Eat a doughnut from a string 148
Play Banned Words 149
Throw a boomerang 150
Play I Spy 151
Learn some board games facts 152
Play How Many Pins...? 154
Play Consequences 155
Play Picture Consequences 156
Play Wink Murder 157

Conclusion 158

INTRODUCTION

We're all guilty of reaching for our phones many more times a day than is necessary—whether it's to settle a debate with a search engine, browse social media, or simply peruse its contents out of boredom. In moderation, this is fine, but too much screen time is not healthy.

So why not set yourself the challenge to use your phone less? You could leave it in another room when you go to bed, so you're not tempted to reach for it as soon as you wake up. Or switch it off when you're engaging in other activities or spending time with friends. You might also find that something as simple as tweaking the settings to offer fewer notifications has you reaching for your device less often.

To help you along the way, this book is here as your handy guide. Animate your interest and stimulate your senses with the host of trivia, activities, experiments, projects, and practical tips in the following pages. Rest those screen-weary eyes and learn something new instead!

NATURE

Whether you've always wanted to teach a parrot to talk, outrun a crocodile, or watch a meteor shower, now is the time to get back to nature.

ATTRACT BUTTERFLIES TO YOUR GARDEN

Butterflies are in decline, so encourage them into your outdoor space. The best way to do this is to present them with flowers in your borders or in pots and hanging baskets. Adult butterflies in general are partial to reds, yellows, oranges, pinks, and purples, so gear your garden towards their floral color preferences. Flowers with tubes are also a plus as they often have the best sources of nectar. Try to stagger the bloom cycles in your garden to attract the winged wonders all year round.

FIGURE OUT WHEN THE SUN IS GOING TO SET

In case you find yourself in a sticky situation out in nature without a watch or phone, you might find this skill useful. First, find a high vantage point where you can see both the sun and the horizon. Avoiding looking at the sun directly, hold your hand up in front of you, palm facing towards you and with your fingers together, and count how many times your hand fits between the sun and the horizon. Use your fingers as fractions if it's not an even number of hands. One hand equals an hour and one finger 15 minutes before sunset.

TEACH A PARROT TO TALK

The top three mimics of the bird world are the African gray parrot, Amazon parrots, and the oft-overlooked budgie. When trying to master the art of bird chat, be patient—repetition is the name of the game and your feathered friend's responses will grow clearer with practice. Set up camp in a quiet room with low lighting, free from distractions, and repeat a word over and over. Alternatively, record your chosen word and play it on a loop. Each bird is different: some will mimic better than others and it's thought that they are more responsive to higher-pitched voices.

BUILD A BIRD FEEDER

1. Take an empty tin can of any size and use an opener to remove the bottom. Use a piece of thick sandpaper to carefully smooth any rough edges.

2. Take a thick piece of cardboard and trace around one end of the tin can, then cut out the circle. Do this twice.

3. Take the cardboard circles and remove the middle third to create a ring.

4. Glue a cardboard ring to each end to cover the edges of the can. This will stop the seed from escaping when the can is hanging.

5. Take two wooden rods or sticks at least half the length of the can and glue to the inside, so that a good amount of the stick protrudes. (You might need to make a hole through the cardboard ring to do this.) These will form perches at either end of your feeder.

6. Tie string around the middle of the can, fill it with bird seed, and hang horizontally from a tree.

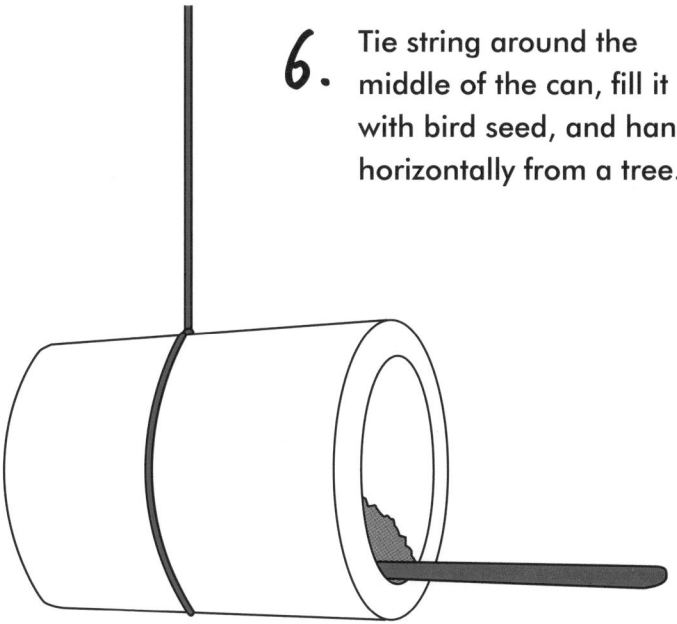

MAKE A NATURAL BIRD FEEDER

Simply take a large, under-ripe pumpkin, hollow it out, fill it with bird food, and hang it from a tree; or use a large pine cone covered with peanut butter and seeds.

WATCH A METEOR SHOWER

For optimum meteor shower viewing you need to get away from artificial light. That means leaving the city and getting away from any built-up areas and into the dark of the countryside. Don't bother with a telescope or binoculars—this massively reduces the amount of sky you can view at any one time and it's all about scanning the great beyond for those elusive shooting stars. Your best bet is the annual Perseid meteor shower, which hits in July/August, and at its peak offers as many as 100 meteors an hour whizzing overhead. Wrap up warm and hope for clear skies!

HOLD A CHICKEN

Many people keep chickens at home, so here is some advice for the next time you visit that bird-keeping friend (or if you get some chickens of your own). Never hold a chicken by its wings. Place its feet side by side and slip the first and second fingers of one hand on either side of them. Keep the chicken's wings folded naturally at its sides and, cupping your hand around the body, use your thumb to cover the primary flight feathers as far as possible. Your other hand can then be placed against the breast to balance the chicken.

GAUGE THE PROXIMITY OF A STORM

During a storm you'll always hear the thunder after the lightning because light travels faster than sound. With the speed of light at 299,792,458 meters per second and the speed of sound 344 meters per second, you can understand why there's quite a delay. Count the seconds between lightning and thunder and multiply by 344 to work out how far away (in meters) the lightning struck. Alternatively, count the number of seconds and divide by five for the number of miles—so 10 seconds between flash and crash would equal 2 miles.

OUTRUN A CROCODILE

While one should never take this up as a sport or try it on a whim, should you ever find you need to escape a crocodile this advice might be useful. Crocodiles are able to move at speeds of up to 11 mph on land, but if you are fit and healthy you should have no problem outrunning the scaly one. Some sources claim crocodiles struggle to change direction quickly, so you could do a bit of zigzagging. However, the fastest route from A to B is in a straight line and crocodiles only experience relatively short bursts of speed, so do what you have to do.

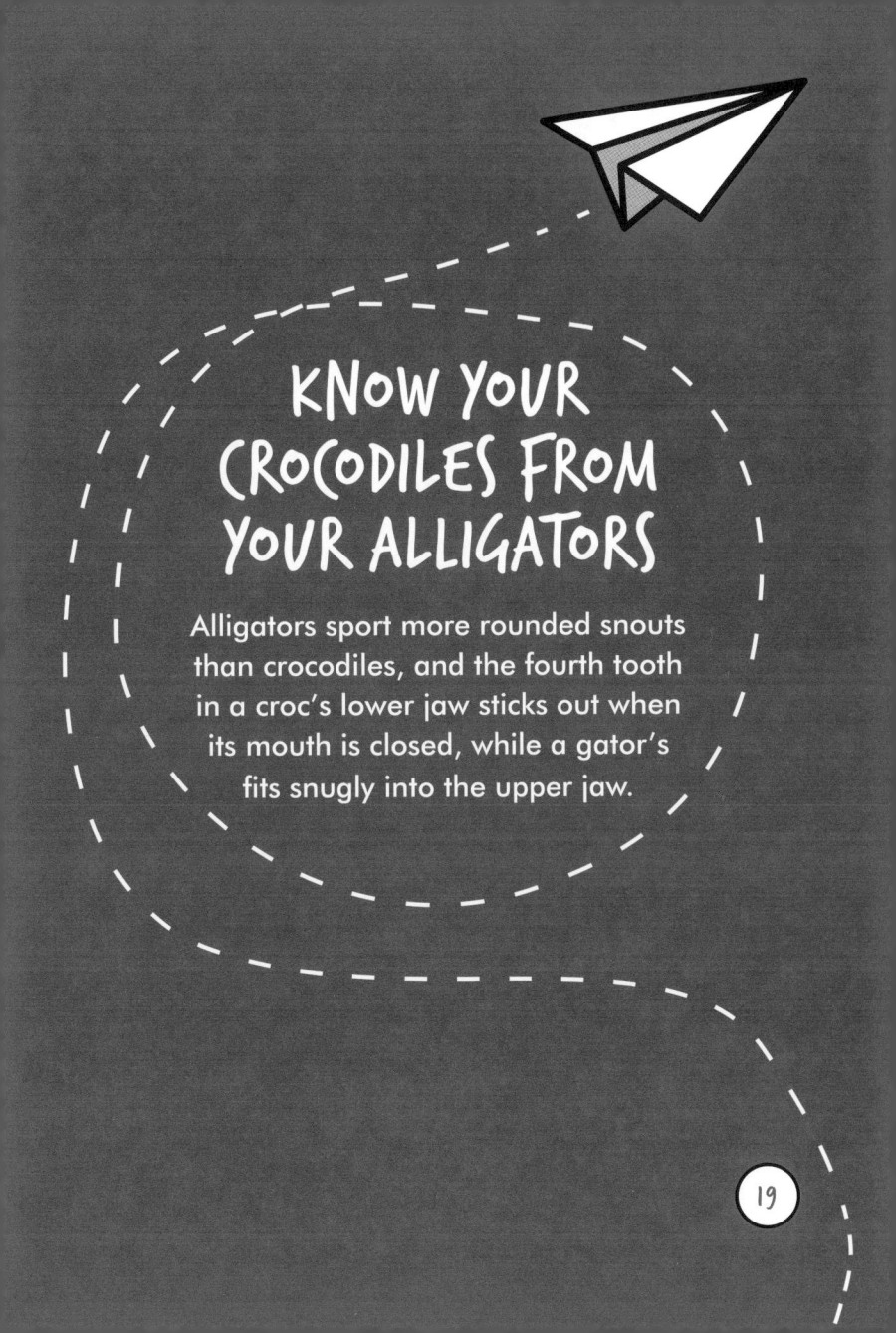

KNOW YOUR CROCODILES FROM YOUR ALLIGATORS

Alligators sport more rounded snouts than crocodiles, and the fourth tooth in a croc's lower jaw sticks out when its mouth is closed, while a gator's fits snugly into the upper jaw.

KNOW YOUR ELEPHANTS

An African elephant has large tusks and ears, a slightly hollowed back, two bumps at the tip of its trunk, and is dark gray; an Asian elephant is lighter gray, smaller, has a slightly arched back, and one bump at the tip of its trunk.

LEARN ANIMAL FAMILY NAMES

How is your knowledge of male, female, and baby animal names? Brush up here.

ANIMAL	MALE	FEMALE	BABY
Goat	Billy	Nanny	Kid
Deer	Buck	Doe	Fawn
Horse	Stallion	Mare	Foal
Sheep	Ram	Ewe	Lamb
Fox	Dog	Vixen	Cub
Seal	Bull	Cow	Pup
Pig	Boar	Sow	Piglet
Bee	Drone	Queen/Worker	Larva
Ferret	Hob	Jill	Kit
Goose	Gander	Goose	Gosling
Hawk	Tiercel	Hen	Eyas
Kangaroo	Buck	Doe	Joey
Duck	Drake	Duck	Duckling
Panda	Boar	Sow	Cub
Wallaby	Jack	Jill	Joey
Whale	Bull	Cow	Calf

KNOW YOUR COLLECTIVE CREATURE NAMES

Bats
A cauldron

Cobras
A quiver

Cockroaches
An intrusion

Crabs
A consortium

Crows
A murder

Eagles
A convocation

Hippos
A thunder

Jaguars
A shadow

Jellyfish
A bloom

Lapwings
A deceit

Larks
An exaltation

Lemurs
A conspiracy

Magpies
A tiding

Otters
A romp

Owls
A parliament

Parrots
A pandemonium

Rhinos
A crash

Squid
An audience

Tigers
An ambush

Salamanders
A maelstrom

Sharks
A shiver

SCIENCE

Ever held a potato in your hand and wondered how to get power from it? Well wonder no more. Here you will also learn how to measure humidity, grow crystals, and build your own volcano.

GET POWER FROM A POTATO

1. Cut a potato in half and cut a small slit into the flat side of each half.

2. Take two pennies and two pieces of copper wire. Wrap a piece of copper wire around each penny a few times.

3. Place a penny into the slit in each potato half.

4. Take another copper wire and wrap it around a zinc-plated nail, then stick the nail into one of the potato halves.

5. Take the wire connected to the penny in the half of potato with the nail and wrap some of it around another nail. Stick that second nail into the other potato half.

6. When you connect the two loose ends of the copper wires to a light bulb or LED it will light up.

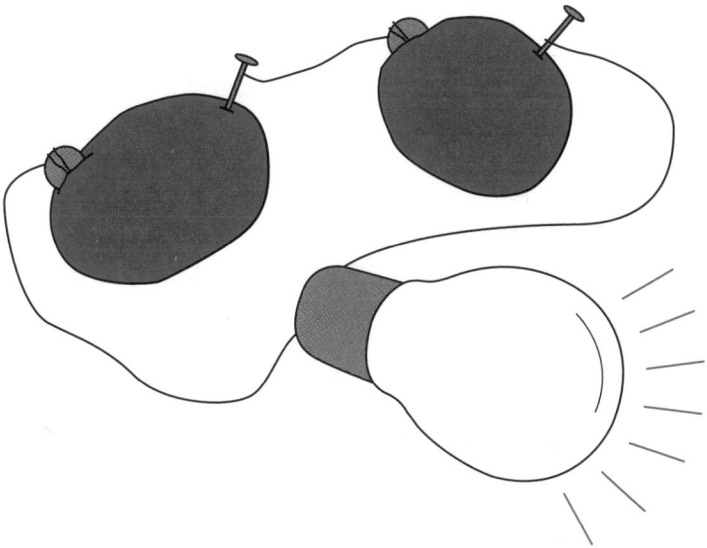

MEASURE HUMIDITY

Human hair gets longer in moist air. So one way of measuring humidity is to fasten a long human hair between two points. If the humidity falls, and the air gets drier, the hair will snap. If it becomes loose then the air has become more humid. The greater the humidity of the air, the more likely it is to rain.

GROW CRYSTALS

Salt, alum, and copper sulphate are good crystal-growing substances to experiment with. (Find alum at your local drugstore and copper sulphate online.) Take a clean jar, fill it two-thirds full of hot water, add some of your substance, and stir until it dissolves. Keep adding and stirring until no more of the substance will dissolve. Tie a piece of string or thread to the middle of a pencil and rest it on the rim of the jar, with the thread dipped into the solution. Leave undisturbed for a week and see the crystals build up on the thread. Add food coloring or ink for more colorful results!

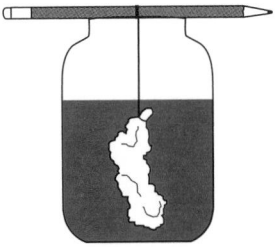

STICK A BALLOON TO THE WALL

This is a good one to impress young children. Take a balloon and rub it against your clothing or hair for 10 seconds to create static, then hold it against a wall and watch how it stays put when you remove your hand.

LEARN THE FIRST 30 ELEMENTS

Hydrogen H	**Sodium** Na	**Scandium** Sc
Helium He	**Magnesium** Mg	**Titanium** Ti
Lithium Li	**Aluminium** Al	**Vanadium** V
Beryllium Be	**Silicon** Si	**Chromium** Cr
Boron B	**Phosphorus** P	**Manganese** Mn
Carbon C	**Sulphur** S	**Iron** Fe
Nitrogen N	**Chlorine** Cl	**Cobalt** Co
Oxygen O	**Argon** Ar	**Nickel** Ni
Fluorine F	**Potassium** K	**Copper** Cu
Neon Ne	**Calcium** Ca	**Zinc** Zn

PLAY GLOW-IN-THE-DARK BOWLING

You'll need six glow sticks, six plastic water bottles (labels removed) nearly full of water, a ball such as a basketball or soccer ball, and something to keep score. Add a glow stick to each bottle (don't forget to replace the tops), set up your "bowling pins" in a triangle formation, and away you go!

WOW YOUR FRIENDS WITH SPACE FACTS

Did you know that if you could find a body of water big enough to hold it, Saturn would float? Saturn is mostly made up of gas and is therefore less dense than water, which would allow it to float, unlike other planets in our solar system which all have higher densities than water. With an impressive diameter of 74,898 miles (120,536 km)—compared with Earth's 7,926 miles (12,756 km)—Saturn is the second largest planet in our solar system behind Jupiter, which has a diameter of a whopping 88,846 miles (142,984 km).

KNOW YOUR BONES

1. Cranium
2. Atlas
3. Mandible
4. Clavicle
5. Scapula
6. Sternum
7. Humerus
8. Vertebrae
9. Radius
10. Ulna
11. Sacrum
12. Coccyx
13. Femur
14. Patella
15. Fibula
16. Tibia

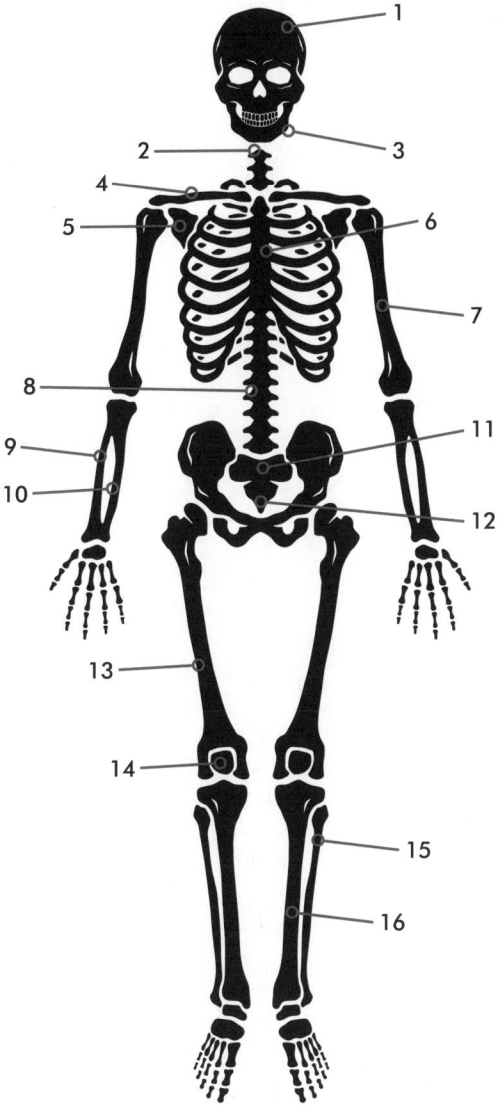
1
2
3
4
5
6
7
8
9
10
11
12
13
14
15
16

MAKE JELLY SET QUICKLY

Need a bowl of jelly in a hurry? Simply add a third less hot water than stated on the packet and top up the jelly mixture with ice. This will bring down the temperature of the mixture quickly and speed up the setting process.

CREATE GIANT BUBBLES

1. Make your own bubble mixture with dish detergent and water in a washing-up bowl. The mixture should comprise approximately three parts water to one part dish detergent, but use trial and error to get your mix right for your type of soap and water. Supercharge it by adding a drop or two of glycerin, available from drugstores and craft shops.

2. To make the wand you'll need two dowel rods about 12 in. long (or you could use two large wooden spoons), some string, and a small weight, like a threaded nut.

3. Cut an approximately 35 in. length of string and thread it through the bolt, and tie the two ends of the string together. Create an upside-down triangle shape with the string with the bolt at the bottom, then attach the top two corners to the ends of your wands with tape.

4. Dip the string into the bubble mixture with the wands together and gently lift out, parting the sticks and waving the string to make your giant bubbles.

MAKE A HOMEMADE VOLCANO

1. Take a large plastic bottle, cut out the middle segment, and reattach the top with tape.
2. Using wet strips of newspaper and glue, build up a volcano shape around the bottle.
3. Once dry, paint it an appropriate color.
4. Now for the eruption—best to move out into the yard for this. Spoon 4 tbsp baking soda into the bottle and, in a separate container, add a few drops of red and yellow food coloring to approximately 1 cup of vinegar.
5. Use a funnel to pour the vinegar into the bottle, but remove the funnel quickly as your eruption will follow soon after!

HISTORY

Wow friends, family, and anyone who will listen with your new-found historical knowledge. From English monarchs and prime ministers to US presidents, not to mention the capital cities of European countries—it's all here for the learning.

MEMORIZE THE ENGLISH MONARCHS

NORMANS

William I
1066–1087

William II
1087–1100

Henry I
1100–1135

Stephen
1135–1154

PLANTAGENETS

Henry II
1154–1189

Richard I
1189–1199

John
1199–1216

Henry III
1216–1272

Edward I
1272–1307

Edward II
1307–1327

Edward III
1327–1377

Richard II
1377–1399

HOUSE OF LANCASTER

Henry IV
1399–1413

Henry V
1413–1422

Henry VI
1422–1461
1470–1471

HOUSE OF YORK

Edward IV
1461–1470
1471–1483

Edward V
1483

Richard III
1483–1485

TUDORS

Henry VII
1485–1509

Henry VIII
1509–1547

Edward VI
1547–1553

Jane Grey
1553

Mary I
1553–1558

Elizabeth I
1558–1603

STUARTS

James I
1603–1625

Charles I
1625–1649

COMMONWEALTH

Oliver Cromwell
1649–1658

Richard Cromwell
1658–1659

STUARTS (restored)

Charles II
1660–1685

James II
1685–1688

William III
1689–1702

Mary II
1689–1694

Anne
1702–1714

HOUSE OF HANOVER

George I
1714–1727

George II
1727–1760

George III
1760–1820

George IV
1820–1830

William IV
1830–1837

Victoria
1837–1901

SAXE-COBURG-GOTHA

Edward VII
1901–1910

WINDSOR

George V
1910–1936

Edward VIII
1936

George VI
1936–1952

Elizabeth II
1952–

BRUSH UP ON YOUR US PRESIDENTS

George Washington
1789–1797

John Adams
1797–1801

Thomas Jefferson
1801–1809

James Madison
1809–1817

James Monroe
1817–1825

John Quincy Adams
1825–1829

Andrew Jackson
1829–1837

Martin Van Buren
1837–1841

William Henry Harrison
1841

John Tyler
1841–1845

James K. Polk
1845–1849

Zachary Taylor
1849–1850

Millard Fillmore
1850–1853

Franklin Pierce
1853–1857

James Buchanan
1857–1861

Abraham Lincoln
1861–1865

Andrew Johnson
1865–1869

Ulysses S. Grant
1869–1877

Rutherford B. Hayes
1877–1881

James A. Garfield
1881

Chester A. Arthur
1881–1885

Grover Cleveland
1885–1889

Benjamin Harrison
1889–1893

Grover Cleveland
1893–1897

William McKinley
1897–1901

Theodore Roosevelt
1901–1909

William Howard Taft
1909–1913

Woodrow Wilson
1913–1921

Warren G. Harding
1921–1923

Calvin Coolidge
1923–1929

Herbert Hoover
1929–1933

Franklin D. Roosevelt
1933–1945

Harry S. Truman
1945–1953

Dwight D. Eisenhower
1953–1961

John F. Kennedy
1961–1963

Lyndon B. Johnson
1963–1969

Richard M. Nixon
1969–1974

Gerald R. Ford
1974–1977

Jimmy Carter
1977–1981

Ronald Reagan
1981–1989

George Bush
1989–1993

Bill Clinton
1993–2001

George W. Bush
2001–2009

Barack Obama
2009–2017

Donald Trump
2017–

KNOW YOUR TWENTIETH- AND TWENTY-FIRST-CENTURY UK PRIME MINISTERS

Marquess of Salisbury
1895–1902

Arthur James Balfour
1902–1905

Henry Campbell-Bannerman
1905–1908

H. H. Asquith
1908–1916

David Lloyd George
1916–1922

Andrew Bonar Law
1922–1923

Stanley Baldwin
1923–1924

Ramsay MacDonald
1924

Stanley Baldwin
1924–1929

Ramsay MacDonald
1929–1935

Stanley Baldwin
1935–1937

Neville Chamberlain
1937–1940

Winston Churchill
1940–1945

Clement Attlee
1945–1951

Winston Churchill
1951–1955

Anthony Eden
1955–1957

Harold Macmillan
1957–1963

Alec Douglas-Home
1963–1964

Harold Wilson
1964–1970

Edward Heath
1970–1974

Harold Wilson
1974–1976

James Callaghan
1976–1979

Margaret Thatcher
1979–1990

John Major
1990–1997

Tony Blair
1997–2007

Gordon Brown
2007–2010

David Cameron
2010–2016

Theresa May
2016–

LEARN ABOUT THE MAJOR CONFLICTS SINCE 1899 THAT INVOLVED THE US

Philippine-American War
1899–1902

The First World War
1914–1918

The Russian Civil War
1917–1922

The Second World War
1939–1945

The Malayan Emergency
1948–1960

The Korean War
1950–1953

The Bay of Pigs Invasion
1961

The Vietnam War
1955–1975

The Gulf War
1990–1991

The Bosnian War
1992–1995

The Kosovo War
1998–1999

The War in Afghanistan
2001–2014

The Iraq War and Insurgency
2003–2011

The Syrian Civil War
2011–

REMEMBER IMPORTANT DATES

There are several handy rhymes to remember important dates in history—try these ones for size:

- In fourteen hundred and ninety-two
  Columbus sailed the ocean blue
  (Christopher Columbus discovers the New World)

- In fifteen hundred and eighty-eight
  the Spanish Armada met its fate
  (the Spanish Armada)

- In sixteen hundred and sixty-five
  scarce a soul was left alive (the Plague)

- In sixteen hundred and sixty-six
  London burned like dried-up sticks
  (the Great Fire of London)

DISCOVER INFLUENTIAL US POLITICIANS AND ACTIVISTS

Benjamin Franklin
1706–1790

John Hancock
1737–1793

John Jay
1745–1829

Alexander Hamilton
c. 1755–1804

Henry Clay
1777–1852

Frederick Douglass
c. 1818–1895

Eleanor Roosevelt
1884–1962

Joseph McCarthy
1908–1957

Shirley Chisholm
1924–2005

Robert F. Kennedy
1925–1968

Martin Luther King Jr.
1929–1968

John McCain
1936–2018

Colin Powell
1937–Present

Madeleine Albright
1937–Present

Geraldine Ferraro
1935–2011

Ruth Bader Ginsburg
1933–Present

Dick Cheney
1941–Present

Hillary Clinton
1947–Present

Al Gore
1948–Present

LEARN ABOUT TOP INVENTORS

- **Thomas Edison** – Invented the phonograph (1877) and motion picture camera (1892)
- **Wright brothers** – Built and flew the first powered aircraft (1903)
- **Benjamin Franklin** – Invented the lightning rod (1749)
- **Nikola Tesla** – Developed modern electricity as we know it (1880s–90s)
- **Konrad Zuse** – Invented the first programmable computer (1941)
- **Alexander Graham Bell** – Credited with inventing the telephone (1876)
- **Leonardo da Vinci** – Inventor of many things that proved workable 500 years later (b. 1452; d. 1519)
- **Galileo** – Developed the telescope (1609)
- **Tim Berners-Lee** – Inventor of the world wide web (1989)

LEARN THE CAPITALS OF EUROPEAN COUNTRIES

Albania
Tirana

Andorra
Andorra la Vella

Armenia
Yerevan

Austria
Vienna

Azerbaijan
Baku

Belarus
Minsk

Belgium
Brussels

Bosnia and Herzegovina
Sarajevo

Bulgaria
Sofia

Croatia
Zagreb

Cyprus
Nicosia

Czech Republic
Prague

Denmark
Copenhagen

Estonia
Tallinn

Finland
Helsinki

France
Paris

Georgia
Tbilisi

Germany
Berlin

Greece
Athens

Hungary
Budapest

Iceland
Reykjavík

Republic of Ireland
Dublin

Italy
Rome

Kosovo
Pristina

Kazakhstan
Astana

Latvia
Riga

Liechtenstein
Vaduz

Lithuania
Vilnius

Luxembourg
Luxembourg

North Macedonia
Skopje

Malta
Valletta

Moldova
Chişinău

Monaco
Monaco

Montenegro
Podgorica

Netherlands
Amsterdam

Norway
Oslo

Poland
Warsaw

Portugal
Lisbon

Romania
Bucharest

Russia
Moscow

San Marino
San Marino

Serbia
Belgrade

Slovakia
Bratislava

Slovenia
Ljubljana

Spain
Madrid

Sweden
Stockholm

Switzerland
Bern

Turkey
Ankara

Ukraine
Kiev

United Kingdom
London

Vatican City
Vatican City

Reykjavik
ICELAND
Murmansk
Arkhangel'sk
FINLAND
SWEDEN
NORWAY
Oslo
Stockholm
Helsinki
St. Petersburg
Tallinn
ESTONIA
RUSSIA
Moscow
Riga
LATVIA
LITHUANIA
Vilnius
Smolensk
Minsk
BELARUS
Edinburgh
Belfast
Dublin
IRELAND
UNITED KINGDOM
London
DENMARK
Copenhagen
Gdansk
Hamburg
Bremen
Berlin
Amsterdam
NETH.
Poznan
Warsaw
POLAND
Kyiv
UKRAINE
Brussels
BEL.
GERMANY
Leipzig
Frankfurt
LUX.
Luxembourg
Prague
CHEH REPUBLIC
Krakow
SLOVAKIA
Bratislava
Paris
Strasbourg
Vienna
Budapesht
Chisinau
MOLDOVA
AUSTRIA
HUNGARY
ROMANIA
FRANCE
Bern
SWITZ.
LIECH.
Vaduz
Geneva
Ljubljana
SLOVENIA
Zagreb
Bucharest
Lyon
Turin
Milan
Bordeaux
CROATIA
BOS. & HERZ.
Belgrad
SERBIA
Toulouse
MONAKO
SAN MARINO
Sarajevo
BULGARIA
Sofia
Pristina
KOS.
MONT.
Istanbul
Porto
ANDORRA
Marseille
Podgorica
Skopje
MACE.
Tirana
ALB.
ITALY
Rome
PORTUGAL
Madrid
Barcelona
Lisbon
SPAIN
Valencia
TURKEY
Izmir
GREECE
Athens
Sevilla
Palermo
MALTA
Valletta

GEOGRAPHY

Ever felt compelled to learn the names of the Hawaiian Islands? Or all the countries in Africa? What about the names of all 50 states or the counties of England? Or how to measure the Earth? Set yourself a few challenges and you'll be surprised at what you can achieve.

KNOW THE TOP 10 LARGEST COUNTRIES BY AREA

COUNTRY	AREA IN SQ MI
Russia	6,601,668
Canada	3,855,102
United States	3,794,100
China	3,705,406
Brazil	3,287,612
Australia	2,988,901
India	1,269,219
Argentina	1,073,518
Kazakhstan	1,052,089
Algeria	919,595

LEARN THE COUNTRIES OF CENTRAL AND SOUTH AMERICA

CENTRAL AMERICA

Belize
Costa Rica
El Salvador
Guatemala
Honduras
Nicaragua
Panama

SOUTH AMERICA

Argentina
Bolivia
Brazil
Chile
Colombia
Ecuador
French Guiana (FRANCE)
Guyana
Paraguay
Peru
Suriname
Uraguay
Venezuela

BELIZE
GUATEMALA
HONDURAS
EL SALVADOR
NICARAGUA
COSTA RICA
PANAMA
VENEZUELA
GUYANA
French Guayana (France)
SURINAME
COLOMBIA
ECUADOR
BRAZIL
PERU
BOLIVIA
PARAGUAY
URUGUAY
ARGENTINA
CHILE

LEARN ALL 50 STATES

ALABAMA
Alaska
Arizona
ARKANSAS
California
Colorado
CONNECTICUT
Delaware
Florida
Georgia
Hawaii
Idaho
ILLINOIS
Indiana
Kansas
KENTUCKY
IOWA
Maryland
Maine
Louisiana
Minnesota
Massachusetts
MICHIGAN
Montana
Mississippi
Missouri
NEW HAMPSHIRE
NEBRASKA
Nevada
New Mexico
New York
NEW JERSEY
Oklahoma
North Carolina
NORTH DAKOTA
Ohio
OREGON
Pennsylvania
Rhode Island
South Carolina
SOUTH DAKOTA
Tennessee
Texas
UTAH
Vermont
VIRGINIA
WEST VIRGINIA
Wisconsin
Washington
WYOMING

WORK YOUR HEAD AROUND POPULATION DENSITY

Did you know that if the entire world were as densely populated as New York City, we would collectively cover 250,404 square miles? This means that everyone would fit into the state of Texas. On the other hand, if everyone were to be spaced out as per the population density in Houston, Texas, we would need 1.77 million square miles in which to live.

NAME ALL OF THE MAIN HAWAIIAN ISLANDS

There are eight Hawaiian Islands—Hawai'i, Kaho'olawe, Kaua'i, Lāna'i, Maui, Moloka'i, Ni'ihau, and O'ahu.

KNOW THE COUNTIES OF ENGLAND

Bath and North East Somerset
BEDFORDSHIRE
Berkshire
Bristol
BUCKINGHAMSHIRE
Cambridgeshire
County Durham
CORNWALL
Cumbria
EAST RIDING OF YORKSHIRE
Derbyshire
Devon
Dorset
East Sussex
Essex
Gloucestershire
GREATER MANCHESTER
HAMPSHIRE
Herefordshire
Hertfordshire
Isle of Wight
Kent
Lancashire
Leicestershire
Merseyside
LINCOLNSHIRE
NORTHAMPTONSHIRE
Norfolk
North Yorkshire
NORTHUMBERLAND
North Somerset
Shropshire
Nottinghamshire
OXFORDSHIRE
Rutland
SOMERSET
South Gloucestershire
Suffolk
South Yorkshire
STAFFORDSHIRE
TYNE AND WEAR
Surrey
WEST MIDLANDS
Wiltshire
West Sussex
WARWICKSHIRE
West Yorkshire
WORCESTERSHIRE

LEARN ABOUT ANTARCTICA

The ice sheet in Antarctica spans a whopping 5.4 million square miles and is the largest solid ice mass on the planet, also making it the home of almost all of the world's fresh water.

MEASURE THE EARTH

The circumference of the Earth around the equator is 24,898 miles. However, if you were to measure the planet's circumference the other way, crossing over the poles, the measurement would be a little less, at 24,812 miles. This is due to the flattening of the Earth at the poles, creating a shape called an oblate spheroid.

KNOW YOUR CONTINENTS

CONTINENT	NO. OF COUNTRIES	FACT
Asia	50	60 percent of Earth's population live here
Africa	55	This is the hottest continent, with the largest desert (the Sahara), which covers 25 percent of Africa.
North America	32	The USA is the largest economy in the world
South America	12	Contains the largest forest (the Amazon rainforest), which covers 30 percent of the continent
Antarctica	1	The coldest continent in the world
Europe	51	The EU is the biggest economic and political union in the world
Australasia or Oceania	14	The least populated continent after Antarctica (only 0.3 percent of the world's population lives here)

LEARN THE COUNTRIES OF AFRICA

Algeria
Angola
Benin
BOTSWANA
Burkina Faso
Burundi
CAMEROON
Cape Verde
Central African Republic
Chad
Comoros
Djibouti
Eritrea
DEMOCRATIC REPUBLIC OF THE CONGO
Equatorial Guinea
Ethiopia
GAMBIA
Ghana
Kenya
Gabon
Côte d'Ivoire
Guinea
LIBERIA
Guinea Bissau
Lesotho
Madagascar
Mauritania
LIBYA
Namibia
Mali
MOROCCO
MALAWI
Mozambique
Nigeria
Mauritius
Republic of the Congo
RWANDA
NIGER
SENEGAL
Réunion
SIERRA LEONE
Somalia
Seychelles
Sao Tome & Principe
SOUTH AFRICA
Sudan
SWAZILAND
Tanzania
Western Sahara
Togo
Tunisia
UGANDA
Zimbabwe
Zambia
ZANZIBAR

KNOW YOUR BODIES OF WATER

There are five oceans on Earth—the Atlantic, Arctic, Indian, Pacific, and Southern oceans—but the term "seven seas" dates back to ancient times and comes from the splitting of the Atlantic and Pacific into the North Atlantic and South Atlantic and North Pacific and South Pacific. When it comes to the other bodies of water across the globe, they include seas, rivers, gulfs, bays, lakes, canals, falls, and straits, and there are too many to count!

INTO THE DEEP

The deepest point on Earth is in the western Pacific, at the southern end of the Mariana Trench, where the ocean reaches depths of 36,200 feet.

WORDS AND LANGUAGE

Rediscover the dying art of postcard writing, learn how to have a bit of banter in Cockney rhyming slang, and pick up Pig Latin to have secretive chats with friends. Better still, make up your own language.

TRY COCKNEY RHYMING SLANG

Adam and Eve
Believe

Apples and pears
Stairs

April showers
Flowers

Barnet Fair
Hair

Battle cruiser
Boozer

Boat race
Face

Brown bread
Dead

Butcher's hook
Look

China plate
Mate

Cream crackered
Knackered

Daisy roots
Boots

Giraffe
Laugh

Jack and Jill
Hill

Lady Godiva
Fiver

Plates of meat
Feet

Pork pies
Lies

Rosie Lee
Tea

Ruby Murray
Curry

Scooby Doo
Clue

Sherbet dab
Cab

Titfer (tit for tat)
Hat

WORLD LANGUAGES

Did you know that there are reportedly over seven thousand languages worldwide, yet approximately half of Earth's population speaks just fifteen languages?

WRITE FLASH FICTION

This is an excellent exercise to get your creative juices flowing and can be done with friends or as a solo mission (although it can be more fun to have people to share the end product with). Set yourself a subject or first line of the story and a time or word limit—an hour or 500 words, whichever you reach first, is a good place to start. Take yourself away from your daily tasks and flex your storytelling muscles.

COMPOSE A HAIKU

A haiku is a Japanese poem that uses sensory language to describe a feeling or experience. They are often inspired by nature, do not rhyme, always consist of three lines, and the syllables always follow the same pattern. The first line should consist of five syllables, the second line seven syllables, and the third line five syllables again. Here's an example:

An old silent pond...
A frog jumps into the pond,
splash! Silence again.

Bashō

SEND A POSTCARD

Whether you're on vacation, on a day trip, or just wandering about locally, send a postcard to someone to show them you're thinking about them. The traditional postcard will always be the best option, but if you want to add a more personal touch you could get postcards printed online using your own photos.

XI LEARN ROMAN NUMERALS

1 I	9 IX	17 XVII	300 CCC
2 II	10 X	18 XVIII	400 CD
3 III	11 XI	19 XIX	500 D
4 IV	12 XII	20 XX	600 DC
5 V	13 XIII	40 XL	700 DCC
6 VI	14 XIV	50 L	800 DCCC
7 VII	15 XV	100 C	900 CM
8 VIII	16 XVI	200 CC	1,000 M

SPEAK PIG LATIN

Pig Latin is used by English-speaking people the world over in situations where they might want to hide something from eavesdroppers—but it will only work if the eavesdroppers don't speak Pig Latin themselves! Simply move the first letter of the word to the end and add "ay." If the word begins with a vowel leave it as it is and add "way." Here are some examples:

Hello – ellohay

Banana – ananabay

Pig Latin – igpay atinlay

Batman and Robin – atmanbay andway obinray

LEARN MORSE CODE

A	. –	S	. . .
B	–. . .	T	–
C	– . – .	U	. . –
D	– . .	V	. . . –
E	.	W	. – –
F	. . – .	X	– . . –
G	– – .	Y	– . – –
H	. . . .	Z	– – . .
I	. .	1	. – – – –
J	. – – –	2	. . – – –
K	– . –	3	. . . – –
L	. – . .	4	. . . . –
M	– –	5	. . . . .
N	– .	6	– . . . .
O	– – –	7	– – . . .
P	. – – .	8	– – – . .
Q	– – . –	9	– – – – .
R	. – .	0	– – – – –

Here is some morse code for you to try your hand at:

a. -.-. --- -. --. .-. .- - ..- .-.. .- - .. --- -. ... /
-.-- --- ..- / -.-. .-. .- -.-. -.- . -.. / - .... . /
-.-. --- -.. .

b. -- --- .-. ... . / -.-. --- -.. . / .-- .- ... / .. -.
...- . -. - . -.. / .. -. / .---- ---.. ...-- -.... /
-... -.-- / .... . -. .-. -.-- / -- --- .-. ... .

c. -- --- .-. ... . / -.-. --- -.. . / -.-. .- -. / -... .
/ - .-. .- -. ... -- .. - - . -.. / --- ...- . .-. / .-.
... -. ..-. .-.. .- / --.- -.... / --- .-. / --- .. -.. -.
.... .. -. --. / .-.. .. --. .... - ...

a. Congratulations you cracked the code
b. Morse code was invented in 1836 by Henry Morse
c. Morse code can be transmitted over radio or by flashing lights

FAMOUS MESSAGES

The most famous messages to be sent via Morse code are "V" (. . . -) for victory, which was sent at the end of World War Two, and "SOS" (. . . - - - . . .).

MOST COMMON LANGUAGES SPOKEN IN HOMES IN THE US

LANGUAGE	NUMBER OF SPEAKERS
English only	229.7 million
Spanish	40.5 million
Chinese (including Mandarin and Cantonese)	3.4 million
Tagalog (including Filipino)	1.7 million
Vietnamese	1.5 million
Arabic	1.2 million
Korean	1.1 million
Russian	1.1 million
German	0.91 million

Aa CREATE YOUR OWN LANGUAGE

A good way to create your own language and then communicate in code among your friends or family is to mix up the alphabet. Come up with a pattern you could use to assign each letter of the alphabet to a new counterpart, for example by flipping the alphabet, so A = Z, B = Y, C = X, etc. Alternatively, you could jump ahead two letters, so A = C, B = D, C = E, etc.

KNOW YOUR BRITISH ENGLISH

Top word(s) = US English
Bottom word(s) = UK English

Barrette
Hair slide

Beet
Beetroot

Cilantro
Coriander

Chips
Crisps

College
University

Cotton candy
Candyfloss

Drugstore
Chemist

Eggplant
Aubergine

Elementary school
Primary school

Elevator
Lift

Emergency room
A&E

First floor
Ground floor

Fish stick
Fish finger

French fries
Chips

Gas
Petrol

Highway
Motorway

Ladybug
Ladybird

Monkey wrench
Spanner

Purse
Handbag

Pants
Trousers

Pacifier
Dummy

Popsicle
Ice lolly

Scallion
Spring onion

Second floor
First floor

Station wagon
Estate car

Thumbtack
Drawing pin

Trunk
Car boot

Vacation
Holiday

Vest
Waistcoat

Zip code
Postcode

Zucchini
Courgette

LEARN SEMAPHORE

A

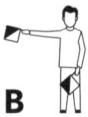
B

C

G

H

I

M

N

O

S

T

U

Y

Z

D

E

F

J

K

L

P

Q

R

V

W

X

KEEP THE ART OF LETTER WRITING ALIVE

The art of letter writing is fast being lost, with emails, text messages, and social media platforms quickly taking over as far swifter forms of communication. Make a point of sending a letter every once in a while and help to keep the practice alive. The recipient will delight in receiving a handwritten or typed missive from you and will most likely sit down and take time out of their day to read about your news.

FOOD

Whether you've always wanted to know how to grow your own name, master chopsticks, or chop onions without crying, it's all here. While you're at it, learn all the plant food families and different pastas, and the very best way to crack a coconut.

PICKLE ONIONS

Take 18 oz. of small shallots, 12 tsp. of salt, 2 cups of malt vinegar, and 7 oz. of clear honey. Place the shallots in a bowl, cover with boiling water and leave to cool. Fish them out with a slotted spoon and trim the roots and tops, then return to the water and sprinkle in the salt. Leave overnight. Rinse the onions and pat dry. Mix the honey and vinegar in a large pan and heat but don't boil. Place the onions into sterilized jars and pour over the honey and vinegar mixture. Add dried chilies/peppercorns for a kick, seal the jars, and leave to cool. The onions will be ready to eat in one month.

KNOW YOUR PLANT FOOD FAMILIES

Umbelliferae – carrots, celery, fennel, parsnips, parsley

Lamiaceae – basil, mint, oregano, sage, thyme

Solanaceae – eggplants, peppers, potatoes, tomatoes

Asteraceae – artichokes, chicory, tarragon, lettuce

Brassicaceae – broccoli, cabbages, cauliflower, watercress

Liliaceae – asparagus, garlic, leeks, onions

Rosaceae – apples, blackberries, raspberries, strawberries

Cucurbitaceae – cucumbers, melons, pumpkins, squashes

Chenopodiaceae – beetroots, chard, spinach

Fabaceae – beans, peas, lentils

Poaceae – barley, corn, oats, rice, wheat

GROW YOUR NAME

On a flat piece of damp cotton or gauze, sprinkle small seeds (cress seeds are ideal) in the shape of the letters of your name. Keep the cotton moist, and in a few days your name will start to grow. An ideal gift for someone who might need cheering up or something for your own kitchen windowsill!

MASTER CHOPSTICKS

Rest the thicker end of one of the chopsticks in the fleshy part of your hand between the base of your thumb and forefinger and hold the lower part of the chopstick between your middle and ring fingers. Place the other chopstick on top and hold between your thumb and forefinger, gripping it halfway along. You should now be able to make a pincer motion with the two chopsticks that will enable you to pick up bits of food and feed yourself. As they say in China, *chī hǎo hē hǎo* (enjoy your meal)!

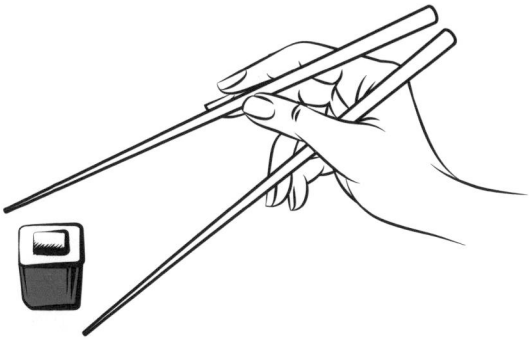

MAKE CHOCOLATE FRIDGE CAKE

1. Melt 11 oz. of dark chocolate in a glass bowl over a saucepan of boiling water.
2. Add 7 tbsp. of butter and ½ cup of corn syrup and stir until smooth.
3. In a separate bowl crush 9 oz. of graham crackers.
4. Add a handful of raisins, candied cherries, and nuts or mini marshmallows to the crackers if you desire.
5. Mix the wet and dry mixtures together and pack into a lined square pan.
6. Place in the fridge for a few hours then remove and cut into squares.

MAKE COOKIES LAST LONGER

Put half a slice of bread into the container; the cookies will absorb the moisture from the bread and stay soft and chewy for longer (make sure to replace the bread after a day or so).

ROAST SWEET CHESTNUTS

There are a few different ways to roast chestnuts and the results are all equally pleasing. Whichever method you choose, be sure to prepare the chestnuts before you cook them—either carefully pierce the skin with a skewer or fork, or cut a slit across the dome of the nut. Then, either shake the nuts in a pan on the stove or place in a dish with a little water and roast for 10 minutes. Add salt or seasoning of your choice and enjoy the sumptuous taste of winter.

CRACK A COCONUT

Ever won a coconut at the summer festival and then found yourself clueless as to how to get at the juicy white flesh? Aside from the chuck-it-at-a-wall method, which isn't the safest or the cleanest, here's how to savor all that lovely coconut without losing an inch of it. Pierce the eyes of the coconut and drain out the milk, then place it in the oven at 350°F for 30 minutes. Leave to cool. If the coconut hasn't cracked on its own, give it a light tap with a hammer.

KEEP FLIES OUT OF YOUR KITCHEN

Grow pots of basil or place bay leaves on your windowsill, and either grow or place bunches of lavender about the room, and flies will stay away.

DRY CHILIES

If you have a bumper crop of chilies, a good way to preserve them for use all year is to dry and string them. They can also look rather colorful in your kitchen. Select as many chilies as you like, and wash and dry them. Thread a needle with flavor-free dental floss or strong thread and make a loop at one end. Insert the needle into the chili near the stem and push it all the way to the loop, then tie a knot. Add as many chilies as you like and hang up in the window. Wait at least three weeks before you use them. Either grind them up and use as chili powder or chop up roughly and add to a bottle of olive oil.

HOW TO MAKE YOUR DRINK COLD QUICKLY

Take a piece of paper towel, run it under the tap to dampen it, wrap it around your drink, and place in the freezer for 15 minutes. You'll be amazed at how quickly it cools down.

MAKE AN EGG STAND UP

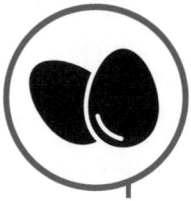

Now for a bit of kitchen "magic." Take an egg and shake it vigorously for 10 seconds to mix up the white and the yolk. Then place the egg on a surface so it is standing upright on its wider end and hold it there for several minutes. During this time the heavier yolk sinks to the bottom of the egg to offer a sturdy base and you will find that eventually the egg stands upright on its own.

KNOW YOUR PASTAS AND HOW TO SERVE THEM

Campanelle – Serve with thick, creamy sauces

Cannelloni – Stuff with meat or veggies and cover in white and tomato sauce

Conchiglie – Stuff the big ones, add the medium-sized to casseroles and the smallest to soups

Farfalle – Make pasta salad or serve with meat and vegetables

Fusilli – Works with all manner of toppings and sauces

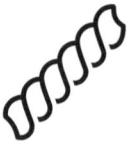

Gnocchi – Serve with rich sauces

Linguine – Use as a spaghetti alternative, serve with seafood or chunky tomato sauce

Macaroni – Performs best in the much-loved macaroni and cheese; add pesto for a greener version

Orzo – Add to soups and salads, or serve hot with vegetables

Pappardelle – Serve with hearty, often meaty, sauces

Penne – Very versatile and goes with most sauces and toppings

Ravioli – Stuff with almost anything and keep it simple with a drizzle of olive oil, or top with cheese or tomato sauce

MAKE YOUR OWN GRANOLA

Preheat the oven to 250°F and line a baking tray with parchment paper. In a large bowl mix approximately 1¾ cups oats, approximately ⅓ cup sunflower seeds, approximately ⅓ cup almond slices/flakes, approximately ⅓ cup dried fruit, ½ tsp cinnamon, ½ tsp salt, ⅓ cup olive oil, and ½ cup maple syrup. Lay the mixture on the baking tray and bake for 40 minutes, turning it over every 10 minutes. Leave to cool and store in a jar.

CHOP ONIONS WITHOUT CRYING

There are several methods you can try to avoid those onion-induced tears. Try freezing the onion for half an hour or submerging it in cold water for a while before you slice it. If that doesn't work, there are specially designed goggles for the job. Slightly wackier but tried and tested: chop the onion with a piece of bread hanging out of your mouth—the bread will absorb the onion gases that cause the tears to flow before they have a chance to reach your eyes.

SPORT AND FITNESS

Learn how to hold a yoga pose and bring about some calm by practicing meditation. There's plenty of trivia here crossing the sports spectrum, along with tips on how to build up to a 5k run and learn some new swimming strokes.

HOLD TREE POSE

This one requires a bit of balance, but you might say it's the "classic" yoga pose.

1. Stand with your feet together and your hands in prayer position.
2. Spread your toes and press them firmly into your mat/the ground.
3. Take one of your feet off the ground and rest the sole either against your other ankle or your inner thigh, if you can manage it, toes pointing to the floor.
4. Keep your breath steady and try not to wobble. Staring at a fixed point can help you to keep your balance.

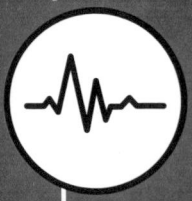

TAKE YOUR OWN PULSE (OR SOMEONE ELSE'S)

Hold out one of your arms, palm up, elbow slightly bent. Using your other hand, place your index and middle finger on the inside of your wrist, at the base of your thumb. Press lightly until you can feel your pulse. Count the number of beats for one minute (or for 30 seconds and multiply it by two). To find your pulse in your neck, press the same fingers on to the side of your neck in the soft hollow below your jaw, next to your windpipe. A healthy resting heart rate for non-athletes should sit between 60 and 100 beats per minute.

LEARN THE TOP TEN MOST DECORATED OLYMPIANS

RANK	NAME	COUNTRY	SPORT
1	Michael Phelps	USA	Swimming
2	Larisa Latynina	Soviet Union	Gymnastics
3	Nikolai Andrianov	Soviet Union	Gymnastics
=4	Boris Shakhlin	Soviet Union	Gymnastics
=4	Marit Bjørgen	Norway	Cross-country Skiing
=4	Takashi Ono	Japan	Gymnastics
=4	Alexei Nemov	Russia	Gymnastics
5	Paavo Nurmi	Finland	Athletics
6	Bjørn Dæhlie	Norway	Cross-country Skiing
7	Viktor Chukarin	Soviet Union	Gymnastics

BUILD UP TO A 5K RUN

Training should take place every other day, three times a week.

Week 1

Brisk 5-minute walk; 1 minute running alternated with 1.5 minutes walking for a total of 20 minutes

Week 2

Brisk 5-minute walk; 1.5 minutes running alternated with 2 minutes walking for a total of 20 minutes

Week 3

Brisk 5-minute walk; two rounds of 1.5 minutes running, 1.5 minutes walking, 3 minutes running, 3 minutes walking

Week 4

Brisk 5-minute walk, 3 minutes running, 1.5 minutes walking, 5 minutes running, 2.5 minutes walking, 3 minutes running, 1.5 minutes walking and 5 minutes running

Week 5

Run one: Brisk 5-minute walk, 5 minutes running, 3 minutes walking, 5 minutes running, 3 minutes walking and 5 minutes running

Run two: Brisk 5-minute walk, 8 minutes running, 5 minutes walking and 8 minutes running

Run three: Brisk 5-minute walk, 20 minutes running with no walking

Week 6

Run one: Brisk 5-minute walk, 5 minutes running, 3 minutes walking, 8 minutes running, 3 minutes walking and 5 minutes running

Run two: Brisk 5-minute walk, 10 minutes running, 3 minutes walking and 10 minutes running

Run three: Brisk 5-minute walk, 25 minutes running with no walking

Week 7

Brisk 5-minute walk, 25 minutes running

Week 8

Brisk 5-minute walk, 28 minutes running

Week 9

Brisk 5-minute walk, 30 minutes running

TOP TEN GOALSCORERS IN MAJOR LEAGUE SOCCER (MLS)

RANK	NAME	GOALS
1	Landon Donovan	145
2	Chris Wondolowski	144
3	Jeff Cunningham	134
4	Jaime Moreno	133
5	Ante Razov	114
6	Kei Kamara	112
7	Jason Kreis	108
8	Bradley Wright-Phillips	106
9	Dwayne De Rosario	104
10	Taylor Twellman	101

EAT A BREAKFAST OF CHAMPIONS

At the height of his career, the most decorated Olympian—swimmer Michael Phelps—was consuming enormous breakfasts to get him through his intensive training regime. Imagine chowing down on the following every day!

- Three fried egg sandwiches with cheese, lettuce, tomatoes, fried onions, and mayonnaise
- Two cups of coffee
- One five-egg omelette
- One bowl of cereal
- Three slices of French toast
- Three chocolate-chip pancakes

Phelps went on to tweak this to a bowl of oatmeal and a large omelette, followed by fruit and coffee.

MEDITATE FOR TEN MINUTES

Meditation is a practice that can help us to relax and focus on the present, driving away unwanted thoughts and worries.

1. Find a quiet space where you won't be interrupted.
2. Sit up straight on the floor with your legs crossed, or in a chair, with your hands on your knees.
3. Close your eyes.
4. Breathe deeply, in through your nose and out through your mouth.
5. Concentrate only on your breath and notice the sensations.
6. If you begin to think about something else, gently steer yourself back to your breath.
7. Do this for 10 minutes every day, or whenever you can, to feel calm and collected.

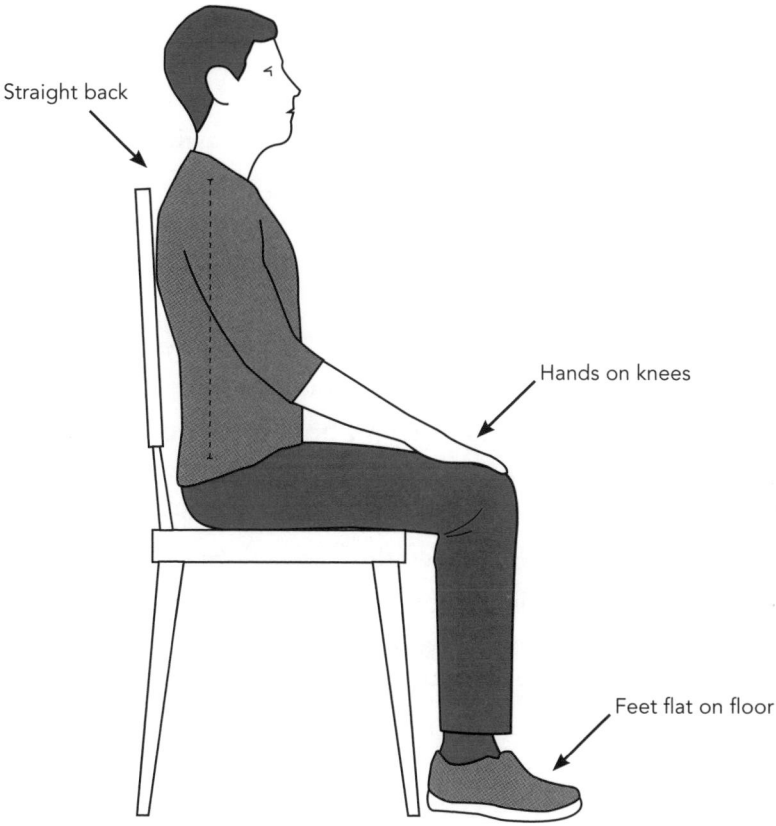
Straight back
Hands on knees
Feet flat on floor

LEARN SOME NEW SWIMMING STROKES

Most of us will be familiar with front crawl, breaststroke, and backstroke, and some of us will even be pretty nifty at butterfly, but why not try one of these styles of swimming to mix things up?

Combat sidestroke – Used by US Navy Seals to swim efficiently and minimize their profile in the water, this involves stretching both arms out in front of you while flutter kicking your legs (as you would in front crawl); your left arm should pull through the water beside you, followed by your right arm, which will automatically tilt you to the side to breathe; at the same time scissor-kick your legs as you would in breaststroke; then reach both arms in front of you again to begin the next stroke.

Trudgen stroke – Used by swimmers to develop both upper and lower-body strength, this involves stretching each arm forward alternately in front of you, a bit like front crawl but keeping your head out of the water, and scissor-kicking your legs (like you would in breaststroke).

Combat sidestroke

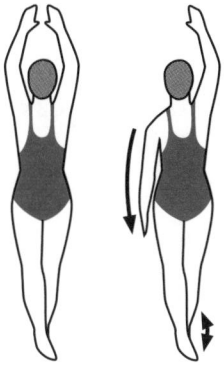

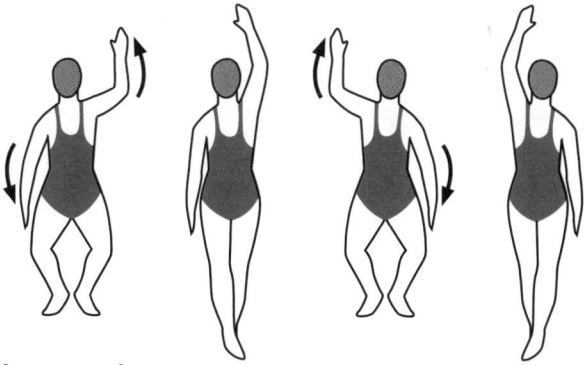

Trudgen stroke

LEARN THE TOP 100 M SPRINTERS

Men

RANK	NAME	NATIONALITY	TIME
1	Usain Bolt	Jamaica	9.58 seconds
2	Tyson Gay	United States	9.69 seconds
3	Asafa Powell	Jamaica	9.72 seconds
4	Maurice Greene	United States	9.79 seconds
=5	Donovan Bailey	Canada	9.84 seconds
=5	Bruny Surin	Canada	9.84 seconds

Women

RANK	NAME	NATIONALITY	TIME
1	Florence Griffith-Joyner	United States	10.49 seconds
2	Carmelita Jeter	United States	10.64 seconds
3	Marion Jones	United States	10.65 seconds
4	Shelly-Ann Fraser	Jamaica	10.73 seconds
5	Christine Arron	France	10.73 seconds

LEARN THE TOP TENNIS GRAND SLAM WINNERS

NAME	COUNTRY	TOTAL WINS
Margaret Court	Australia	24
Serena Williams	USA	23
Steffi Graf	Germany	22
Roger Federer	Switzerland	20
Helen Wills Moody	USA	19
Chris Evert	USA	18
Martina Navratilova	USA	18
Rafael Nadal	Spain	16
Pete Sampras	USA	14
Novak Djokovic	Serbia	14
Roy Emerson	Australia	12
Billie Jean King	USA	12

KNOW YOUR FIFA WORLD CUP WINNERS

YEAR	WINNER
1982	Italy
1986	Argentina
1990	West Germany
1994	Brazil
1998	France
2002	Brazil
2006	Italy
2010	Spain
2014	Germany
2018	France

STEP IT UP

Wearable fitness trackers typically recommend a daily goal of 10,000 steps to keep fit and healthy, and this roughly translates to around 5 miles. If that's too much for you, set your sights a bit lower and try to achieve your goal each day before working your way up. The benefits of walking are many, with fresh air and exercise not only being essential to general health and well-being, but also likely to have a positive effect on your mood.

THE ARTS

Whether you've always wanted to master the nose flute or learn how to make one of those cute origami birds, look no further. Master the art of drawing faces, make marbled paper, and memorize the best-selling albums of all time while clicking away on the castanets.

LEARN THE FIVE MOST EXPENSIVE WORKS OF ART SOLD AT AUCTION

ARTIST	WORK OF ART	SALE PRICE	AUCTION DATE
Leonardo da Vinci	*Salvator Mundi (Savior of the World)*	$450 million	2017
Pablo Picasso	*Les Femmes d'Alger (Women of Algiers)*	$179 million	2015
Amedeo Modigliani	*Nu Couché (Reclining Nude)*	$170 million	2015
Francis Bacon	*Three Studies of Lucian Freud*	$142 million	2013
Edvard Munch	*Skrik (The Scream)*	$120 million	2012

MAKE AN ORIGAMI BIRD

1. Take a square piece of paper (origami paper will look the nicest) and fold the top corner to the bottom corner.

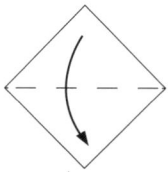

2. Now fold the left corner over to the right corner.

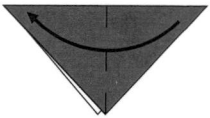

3. Open the top flap and fold the top corner to meet the bottom corner; then flip over and do the same on the other side.

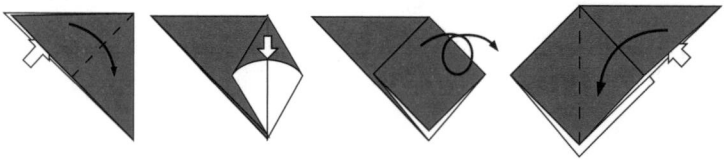

4. On one side, fold the left and right corners to meet in the center and fold down the top triangle.

5. Unfold step 4 and open up the top layer, using the creases as guides fold the left and right sides into the center. Do the same on the other side.

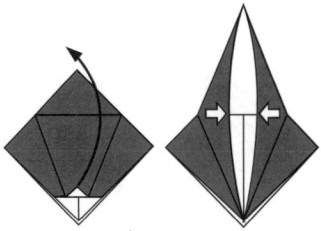

6. Take the top layer from the right side and fold it to the left. Do the same on the other side.

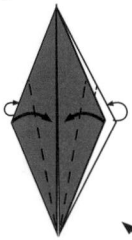

7. Take the bottom corner of the top layer and fold it up. Do the same on the other side.

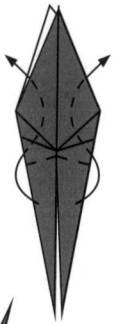

8. Take hold of the two wedges in the middle and pull them out to the sides. Crease along the bottom to hold these in place.

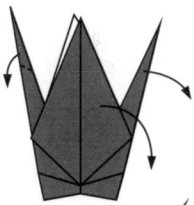

9. Open the left wedge and fold it in on itself to create the bird's head, fold the wings down and voilà!

DRAW A FACE

1. Using a pencil, draw the shape of the head.

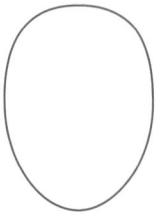

2. Halfway from the top, lightly draw a horizontal line (this is where the eyes will go).

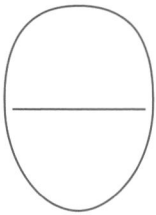

3. Lightly draw a vertical line down the middle (this will help to keep the features in the right place).

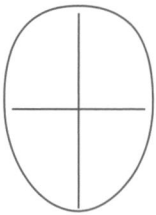

4. Halfway between the eye line and the chin, draw a short line (this will become the nose).

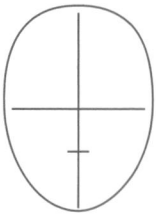

5. Slightly above the halfway point between the nose and chin draw a longer line (this will become the mouth).

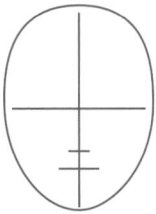

6. Using an art pencil or pen for the next steps, draw two curves on the eye line and then study the eyes you are drawing and adjust the shape accordingly below the line. See the example on this page.

7. Draw on a nose and mouth using your guide lines. Then add hair and remember it needs to sit above and below the skull outline.

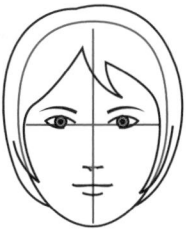

8. Erase all your pencil guidelines and there you have it.

MASTER THE NOSE FLUTE

You don't need much musical experience to play this instrument, so why not give it a try? Press the smaller end of the flute against your nose and the larger end against your mouth. Form a seal with the instrument around your nostrils, but keep your mouth open slightly. Only breathe out through your nose and as you begin to create tunes, alter the shape of your mouth as you exhale through your nose to vary the pitch.

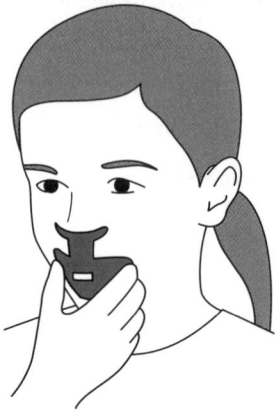

LEARN TO PLAY THE CASTANETS

Do your best flamenco impression with these easy-to-follow instructions. Take the castanets and place one in each hand. Thread your thumb through the loop so your thumb sits on the outside and you can use your other fingers to click the plates together. Your left hand should play a simple rhythm while your right takes on the more complicated rhythm of the dance. See how you get on!

CHANGE THE COLOR OF A FLOWER

Ever had a hankering for a bunch of blue roses but never see them at the local florist? Well here's how you can make your own. Buy some pale roses—white or cream will work best—and place the stems into a strong solution of blue ink or food coloring and water (or whatever color you desire). The rose will "drink" the ink and eventually change color. Try making a multi-colored rose by splitting the stem in half and placing each half into a different-colored solution.

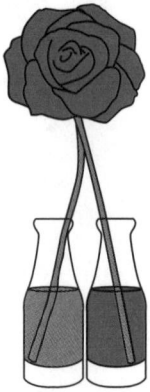

TAKE A GREAT PHOTOGRAPH

Rediscover the lost art of taking a photograph with these handy tips.

Focus – Make sure your subject matter is looking sharp.

Lighting – Always think about the light. Sunlight overhead can cast shadows and the sun behind you will make people squint. Play around with different positions to find the perfect spot.

Horizon – Always keep it straight!

Perspective – Create a sense of depth and perspective by including items in the foreground of your photograph.

Natural lines – Whether these are in the clouds, trees, roads, or buildings, or are horizontal, vertical, or zigzag, lines will guide the viewer's eyes around your photograph.

LEARN THE TOP 10 BEST-SELLING ALBUMS OF ALL TIME

ARTIST	ALBUM	YEAR	SALES
Michael Jackson	*Thriller*	1982	66 million
AC/DC	*Back in Black*	1980	50 million
Pink Floyd	*The Dark Side of the Moon*	1973	45 million
Whitney Houston/ Various artists	*The Bodyguard*	1992	45 million
Meat Loaf	*Bat Out of Hell*	1977	43 million
Eagles	*Their Greatest Hits (1971–1975)*	1976	42 million
Bee Gees/ Various artists	*Saturday Night Fever*	1977	40 million
Fleetwood Mac	*Rumours*	1977	40 million
Shania Twain	*Come On Over*	1997	39 million
Led Zeppelin	*Led Zeppelin IV*	1971	37 million

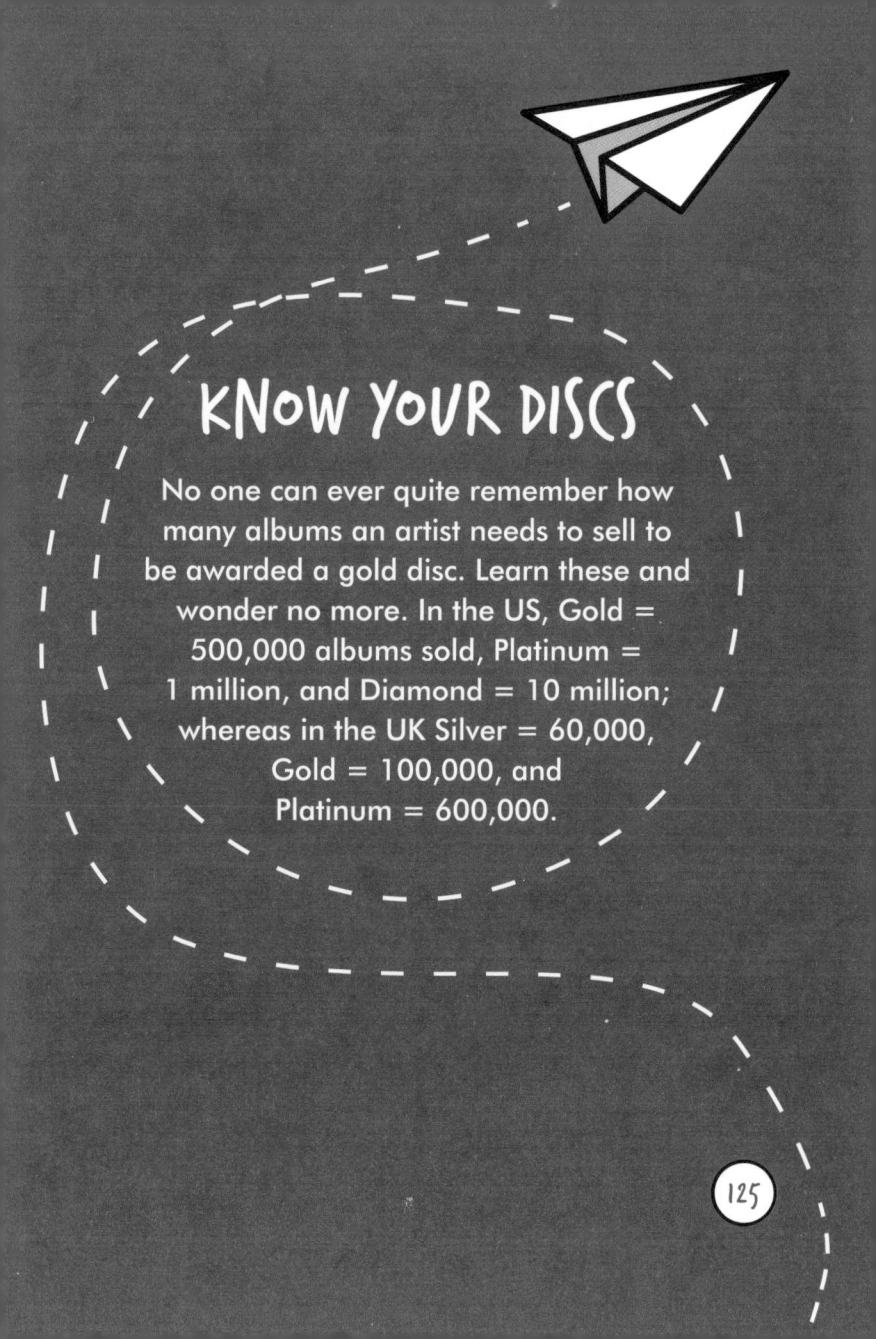

KNOW YOUR DISCS

No one can ever quite remember how many albums an artist needs to sell to be awarded a gold disc. Learn these and wonder no more. In the US, Gold = 500,000 albums sold, Platinum = 1 million, and Diamond = 10 million; whereas in the UK Silver = 60,000, Gold = 100,000, and Platinum = 600,000.

CREATE MARBLED PAPER

1. Take a large foil tray or casserole dish—something that will fit your desired paper size.
2. Add water to the tray to fill it 1–2 cm from the bottom.
3. Take a few different colors of nail polish or ink and add a few drops of each to the surface of the water.
4. Using a pin or knitting needle, move the water around gently to create a marbling effect.
5. Place your paper carefully onto the surface of the water—don't let it go under.
6. Take a corner of the paper and gently lift it away from the water.
7. Leave it to dry and then admire your creation!

KNOW YOUR RECENT PULITZER PRIZE FOR FICTION WINNERS

DATE	RECIPIENT	TITLE OF WORK
2008	Junot Díaz	*The Brief Wondrous Life of Oscar Wao*
2009	Elizabeth Strout	*Olive Kitteridge*
2010	Paul Harding	*Tinkers*
2011	Jennifer Egan	*A Visit From the Goon Squad*
2012	N/A	N/A
2013	Adam Johnson	*The Orphan Master's Son*
2014	Donna Tartt	*The Goldfinch*
2015	Anthony Doerr	*All the Light We Cannot See*
2016	Viet Thanh Nguyen	*The Sympathizer*
2017	Colson Whitehead	*The Underground Railroad*
2018	Sean Greer	*Less*

LEARN THE BESTSELLING FICTION BOOKS OF ALL TIME

TITLE	AUTHOR	SALES
Don Quixote (1605)	Miguel de Cervantes	500 million
A Tale of Two Cities (1859)	Charles Dickens	200 million
The Lord of the Rings (1954–5)	J. R. R. Tolkien	150 million
The Little Prince (1943)	Antoine de Saint-Exupéry	140 million
Harry Potter and the Philosopher's Stone (1997)	J. K. Rowling	120 million
The Hobbit (1937)	J. R. R. Tolkien	100 million
And Then There Were None (1939)	Agatha Christie	100 million
Dream of the Red Chamber (1754)	Cao Xueqin	100 million
Alice's Adventures in Wonderland (1865)	Lewis Carroll	100 million
The Lion, the Witch and the Wardrobe (1950)	C. S. Lewis	85 million

ETIQUETTE

From getting the knack of tying a bow tie, to walking in heels, dressing appropriately for an occasion, and laying the table for the perfect dinner party, you can learn it all here.

WEAR FLOWERS IN YOUR HAIR

Take a plain, thin headband, preferably one that matches the color of your hair, and customize it to your heart's desire. Create a flower crown with three or four large flowers in a row in the center, or opt for a day-at-the-races-style fascinator with a stylish large, white flower off to the side with a bit of black netting underneath to add a touch of class.

MAKE DECORATIVE FLAGS FROM OLD CLOTHES

You can do this with any items of clothing, but you might find dresses or jazzy shirts offer the most suitable material, as well as interesting patterns. Cut triangles out of your clothing and sew on to a long strip of wide ribbon, folding the ribbon over the top of the short side of the triangles as you sew. For fuller bunting, sew the triangles together inside out and then reverse before sewing to the ribbon. String up for an instant party vibe.

TIE A BOW TIE

The bow tie originated in Croatia in the seventeenth century to hold one's shirt collar together.

1. Place the bow tie round your neck. The left side should be about an inch longer than the right. Cross the left side over the right side.

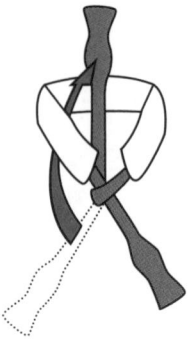

2. Wrap the longer side of the bow tie around the shorter, and up through the loop. Hold it up straight.

3. Fold the shorter end of the tie in half horizontally.

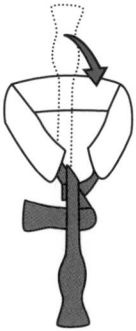

4. Bring the longer end of the tie down in front of the shorter, folded end.

5. Insert it through the loop at the back of the shorter section of tie.

6. Pull both ends gently to tighten and adjust the knot.

LAY A TABLE FOR A DINNER PARTY

There is a lot to remember when it comes to laying the table for a posh dinner party.

1. First start with the plate. It's likely you will plate up in the kitchen, but it's best to have something to work around.

2. Lay forks to the left of the plate and knives to the right in the order they will be used, working inwards. Place the salad knife and fork first.

3. Next place the meat fork on the left and the meat knife on the right, followed by the fish fork and knife.

4. Place the dessert fork above the plate in a horizontal position with the handle facing left and the dessert spoon above the fork with the handle facing right.

5. Finally add a side plate for bread to the left of the forks and water and wine glasses in the right-hand corner of the place setting.

Dessert spoon
Dessert fork
Fish fork
Salad fork
Meat fork
Salad knife
Fish knife
Meat knife

WALK IN HEELS

Straighten your back and place your heel on the ground first, followed by your toes. When your weight is on the ball of your foot, shift your weight forwards as if you are walking on your tiptoes, push forwards and then take your next step.

LEARN ABOUT TIPPING PRACTICES

Tipping practices are different across the world. In the UK, a service charge (which is not counted as a tip) is often not automatically added, and the traditional "tip" is 10 percent, to be shared between the party. Some restaurants specify on the receipt if an obligatory service charge is included in the bill; in these cases it is usually 12.5 percent, and your tip is a bonus for the staff on top of that. When you are abroad, make sure you are familiar with the dos and don'ts of the country's service culture as these can often differ wildly from your own. You don't want to be chased down the street for tipping incorrectly!

WEAR A SILK SCARF

1. Fold in half to create a triangle, roll over the top and tie around your neck at the back, cowboy/girl style.

2. Roll it out and tie around your neck with the knot at the side, for Parisian chic.

3. Roll it up and place on your head like a headband, tying it underneath your loose hair, for a retro, 1950s look.

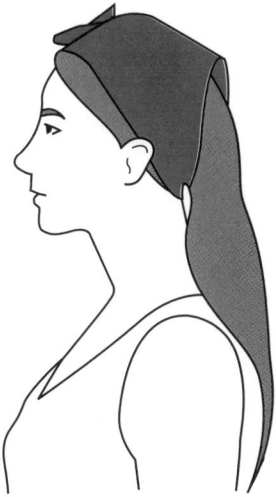

4. Fold as in no. 1 and place over your head, tying under your hair for a 1990s vibe.

5. Reverse number 1 so the scarf is tied at the front, for a country living feel.

DRESS FOR THE OCCASION

Black tie – A black dinner jacket, matching dress pants, a white shirt, and black bow tie; or an evening gown, traditionally floor-length.

Business formal – A suit or smart shirt and formal dress pants or skirt, with discreet, if any, accessories.

Smart/casual – Generally means to dress in casual clothes, but with none of the following: T-shirts, denim, sneakers, or beachwear.

SEND THANK-YOU NOTES

Within a couple of days of attending a wedding, party, or any kind of event hosted by someone else, make sure you send a thank-you note. These days many people will opt for a thank-you text message or note via social media, but let's keep the art of letter writing alive by popping something in the mail. Have a box of thank-you notes or cards ready for such occasions (or make your own!) and the act will always be remembered.

MAKE MOCKTAILS

Virgin Mojito

Ingredients

5 mint leaves plus extra to garnish
1 tbsp fresh lime juice
1 tsp sugar
Crushed ice
8.5 fl. oz. ginger ale, soda water, or lemonade
Slice of lime to garnish

Method

Place the mint leaves, lime juice, and sugar in a tall glass and muddle well. Add a spoonful or two of crushed ice and top up with ginger ale, soda water, or lemonade, depending on how sweet you want the end result to be. Give the whole lot a good stir and then top up with more crushed ice, if needed, and a sprig of mint and a slice of lime to garnish.

Mango Fizz

Ingredients

5 mint leaves plus extra to garnish
1 fl. oz. mango purée
1 fl. oz. lime juice
1 fl. oz. sugar syrup
Crushed ice
4 fl. oz. ginger ale
Slice of lime to garnish

Method

Place the mint, sugar syrup, and mango purée in a tall glass and muddle gently. Add a handful or two of crushed ice, until the glass is two-thirds full, and top up with ginger ale. Give the whole thing a good stir, add more crushed ice, if needed, and garnish with a sprig of mint and a slice of lime.

BE THE PERFECT HOST

- On arrival, take coats and offer guests a drink
- Offer non-drinkers their libation in a wine glass where appropriate
- Make sure there are snacks or canapés on hand to go with the first drink
- Ensure you have prepared sufficiently so that you do not spend all your time in the kitchen and that the time between courses does not drag
- Keep music at a light volume so voices do not need to be raised
- Ensure all dietary requirements have been taken care of
- Match drinks to courses and explain to guests what they are eating and drinking
- Make sure you have a selection of teas and coffees for those who prefer something a bit different.

GAMES

Can you eat a doughnut without licking your lips? And how's your poker face? Here you will learn how to play it cool so you don't give the game away to your opponents, as well as how to master a host of new games and activities.

TURN RIGHT

For this activity, all you need is yourself. The rules are simple: go outside and start walking. Each time you reach a junction you can only keep going forward or turn right. It's deceptively simple—this is a great way to discover something new. You may even find a hidden gem of a place right round the corner! Try this in a car or on a bike if you want to travel further.

KEEP A POKER FACE

The key to a good poker game is keeping your hand to yourself. It's human nature to show emotion on your face when you get a good or bad hand, so the first rule is to put a stop to that. First you need to concentrate on relaxing your face and be mindful to keep it relaxed. Make sure you maintain good eye contact with the other players and blink occasionally—don't stare. Relax your posture, keep your words to a minimum, and reply calmly when spoken to. Good luck!

EAT A DOUGHNUT FROM A STRING

This is a good one for Halloween (or any time you want to have a little fun) and is a real test for your self-control. Sugared ring doughnuts are best for this game as they are easy to attach. Simply thread each doughnut onto the string, then tie the string between two points, making sure it's high enough that the dangling doughnuts will be roughly at mouth height. Then let the players battle it out. You may not, under any circumstances, lick your lips until every bit of the doughnut has been swallowed.

PLAY BANNED WORDS

This game works best over the course of a meal, evening or weekend. Choose a word or phrase that is off limits for the duration of the time you will spend with the players. This could be anything from "bathroom" or "kitchen" to someone's name or an event or place. Whoever drops the banned word over the course of the game needs to then perform a forfeit.

THROW A BOOMERANG

When we think of a boomerang we tend to think of it returning—and although a boomerang can perform this trick, it isn't how it was traditionally used (which was as a weapon for hunting). In order to throw a boomerang and have it return to you, you need to hold the boomerang vertically, gripping it at the end of the bottom "wing." The nose of the boomerang should be facing out away from you. Then take the boomerang behind you and let go of it as if you were throwing a baseball.

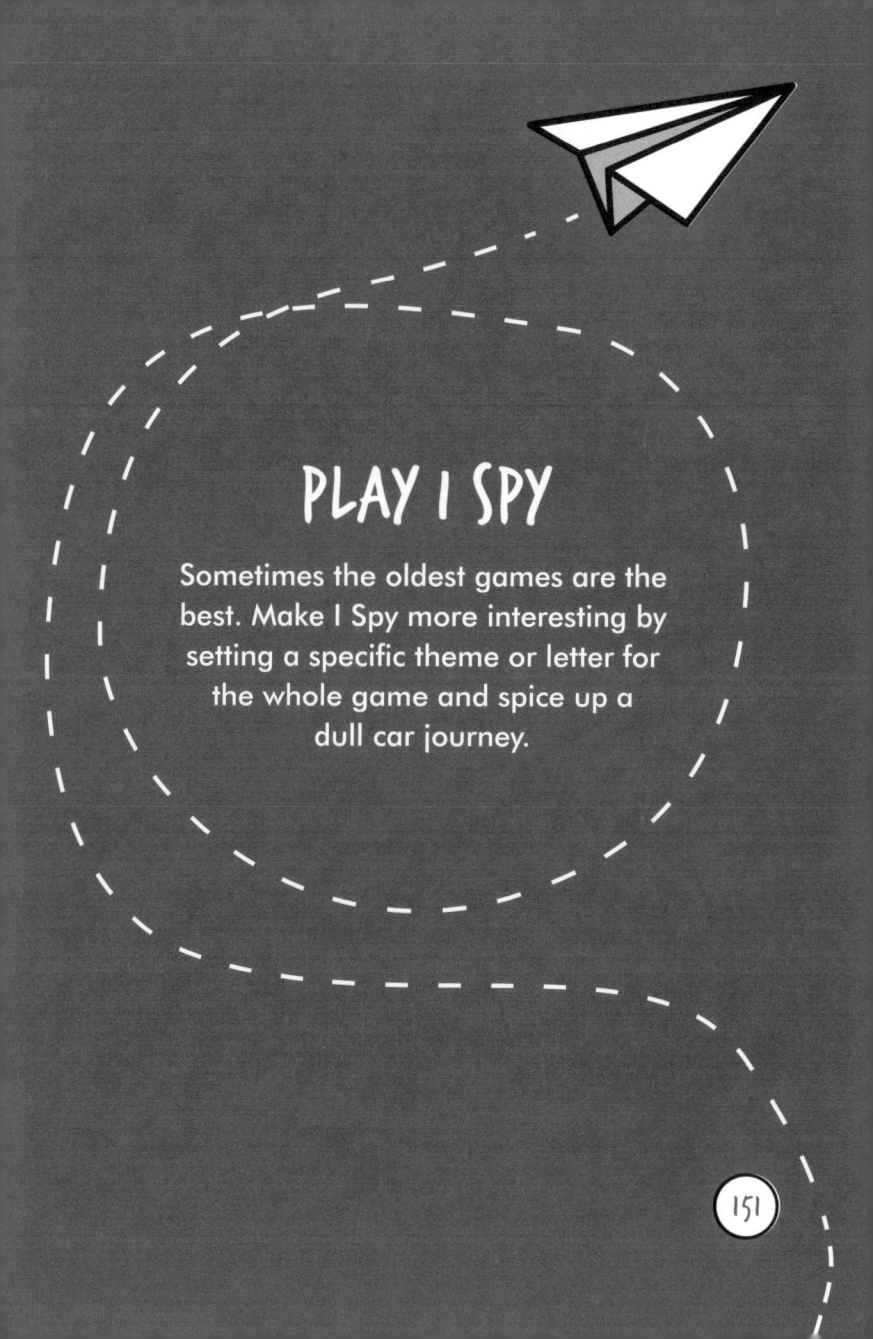

PLAY I SPY

Sometimes the oldest games are the best. Make I Spy more interesting by setting a specific theme or letter for the whole game and spice up a dull car journey.

LEARN SOME BOARD GAMES FACTS

- The longest game of Monopoly ever played lasted 70 days.

- The Monopoly mascot used to be called Rich Uncle Pennybags before it was changed to Mr. Monopoly.

- Snakes and Ladders originated in India in the nineteenth century, with the snakes and ladders representing karma—destiny and desire, respectively.

- Clue, originally called "Murder!", was patented in 1947 but wasn't produced until 1949 due to post-war shortages. Original weapons included a bomb, syringe, and fireplace poker.

- The highest score ever recorded for a word in Scrabble was 392 with "caziques" (tropical Central American/South American birds) and the highest score for a game was 1,049.

- Scrabble was originally called "Lexico."

- Jenga is Swahili for "build" and the game has sold more than 50 million copies, which equates to over 2.7 billion bricks.

- Trivial Pursuit was invented by two Canadians who found there were tiles missing from their Scrabble set and so made up their own game.

- Chess originated in India around AD 280–550 and the pawns, knights, bishops, and rooks were originally infantry, cavalry, elephants, and chariotry.

PLAY HOW MANY PINS...?

Sort of like human Buckaroo, the object is to see how many clothespins you can attach to other players over the course of a day or evening without them realizing. Whoever secures the most pins wins the game. This is a good one to play alongside another game, so everyone is distracted. Buy pins in a selection of sizes and assign a points system, so giant pins score the highest and miniature pins score less. Ask players to write their initials on their assigned pins.

PLAY CONSEQUENCES

Each player needs a piece of paper and a pen. This game has six rounds and between each round the paper will be passed to the player on the left. Each player should first write the name of a person, fold over the paper enough to cover what they have written, and pass it on. Then should come the name of another person, a place (where they met), then what person 1 says to person 2, then what person 2 says back, then the consequence (what happened next). Each time something is written, the paper is folded over enough to cover it. Pass it on a final time, unfold, and read out to much hilarity.

PLAY PICTURE CONSEQUENCES

Try the above, but with pictures instead and three rounds—one each for the head, the middle, and the bottom half—nothing is off limits, so animals/monsters/humans are all welcomed.

PLAY WINK MURDER

This is best played around a dinner table or at a party when people are distracted by conversation. Assign the murderer by placing as many pieces of paper in a hat as there are players, including one with the word "murderer" on it. The murderer should then wink at other players to kill them off. Players that are still alive can accuse if they suspect. A victorious murderer will most likely kill all players but one!

CONCLUSION

As you've made it this far, I hope the preceding pages have demonstrated just how limitless the options are when it comes to reducing your screen time and doing something more imaginative, stimulating, and hands on! As incredible as modern technology has become, it's important to remember that there is a balance to be struck between being entertained by gadgets and doing things that can get us moving and thinking in different ways. Try learning something new every day and you'll be surprised at what you can achieve.

IMAGE CREDITS

p.3 © bounward/Shutterstock.com; p.8 © Pensiri/Shutterstock.com; p.9 © goodzone/Shutterstock.com; p.11 © alexcoolok/Shutterstock.com; p.12 © Vector Market/Shutterstock.com; pp.12-13 © Hamish braid; p.14 © bounward/Shutterstock.com; p.15 © father/Shutterstock.com; p.16 © Ivan Lukyanchuk/Shutterstock.com; p.17 © Reservoir Dots/Shutterstock.com; p.18 © Margarita L/Shutterstock.com; p.19 © bounward/Shutterstock.com; p.20 © bounward/Shutterstock.com; p.21 © Lillyy/Shutterstock.com; p.22 © Big Clouds team/Shutterstock.com; p.23 © Moofer/Shutterstock.com; p.24 © AF studio/Shutterstock.com; p.25 © Hamish braid; p.26 © Illustration Projects/Shutterstock.com; p.27 © F16-ISO100/Shutterstock.com; p.28 © veronchick84/Shutterstock.com; p.29 © notbad/Shutterstock.com; p.31 © Panptys/Shutterstock.com; p.32 © Rashad Ashurov/Shutterstock.com; p.33 © Maks TRV/Shutterstock.com; p.34 © quka/Shutterstock.com; p.35 © Hamish Braid; p.36 © In-Finity/Shutterstock.com; p.37 © tulpahn/Shutterstock.com; p. 38 © anpannan/Shutterstock.com; p.40 © vector toon/Shutterstock.com; p.42 © Puckung/Shutterstock.com; p.44 © IconBunny/Shutterstock.com; p.45 © Alexandr III/Shutterstock.com; p.46 © Cube29/Shutterstock.com; p.47 © Vector Market/

Shutterstock.com; p.48 © Cube29/Shutterstock.com; p.49 kosmozoo/Gettyimages.com; p.50 © LovArt/Shutterstock.com; p.51 © Arcady/Shutterstock.com; p. 52 © Arcady/Shutterstock.com; p. 53 © PytyCzech/iStockphoto.com; p.54 © imMadchi/Shutterstock.com; p.55 © supanut piyakanont/Shutterstock.com; p.56 © bounward/Shutterstock.com; p.57 © artolegg/Shutterstock.com; p.58 © Day Of Art/Shutterstock.com; p 59 © Fine Art/Shutterstock.com; p.60 © Pensiri/Shutterstock.com; p.61 © AF studio/Shutterstock.com; p.62 © Kurdanfell/Shutterstock.com; p.63 © bounward/Shutterstock.com; p.64 © AVIcon/Shutterstock.com; p.65 © fad82/Shutterstock.com; p.66 © bounward/Shutterstock.com; p.67 © Rashad Ashurov/Shutterstock.com; p.68 © Daria Sokolova/Shutterstock.com; p.69 © justone/Shutterstock.com; p.70 © shuvector/Shutterstock.com; p.71 © Visual Generation/Shutterstock.com; p.72 © ElsayedKaram/Shutterstock.com; p.74 © bounward/Shutterstock.com; p.75 © Arcady/Shutterstock.com; p.77 © stockish/Shutterstock.com; p.78 © LWY Partnership/Shutterstock.com; pp.78-79 © Evgenii Bobrov/Shutterstock.com; p.80 © Magic Pasta/Shutterstock.com; p.81 © veronchick84/Shutterstock.com; p.82 © Pavel K/Shutterstock.com; p.83 © Ice_AisberG/Shutterstock.com; p.84 © Rimma Rii/Shutterstock.com; p.85 © MSSA/Shutterstock.com; p.86 © Oleh Markov/Shutterstock.com; p.87 © bounward/Shutterstock.com; p.88 © Cube29/Shutterstock.com; p.89 © Happy Art/Shutterstock.com; p.90 © bounward/Shutterstock.com; p.91 © amfoto/Shutterstock.com; p.92 © bounward/Shutterstock.com; p.93 © Maxim Cherednichenko/Shutterstock.com; p.94 © Farah Sadikhova/Shutterstock.com; p.94 – gnocchi © Dn Br; campanelle, cannelloni, conchiglie, farfalle, fusilli © Alexandr III/Shutterstock.com; p.95 – orzo © stockakia; linguine, macaroni, pappardelle, penne, ravioli © Alexandr III/Shutterstock.com; p.96 © RedKoala/Shutterstock.com; p.97 © vectorchef/Shutterstock.com; p.98 © Redberry/Shutterstock.com; p.99 © Stock Vector/Shutterstock.com; p.100 © DStarky/Shutterstock.com; p.101 © Classica2/Shutterstock.com; p.102 © HuHu/Shutterstock.com; p.104 © D Line/Shutterstock.com; p.105 © Vector Tradition SM/Shutterstock.com; p.106 © Pavel K/Shutterstock.com; p.107 © Hamish Braid; p.108 © Businessvector/Shutterstock.com; p.109 © Guaxinim/Shutterstock.com; p.110 © puruan/Shutterstock.com; p.111 © saravector/Shutterstock.com; p.112 © vectorEps/Shutterstock.com; p.113 © nelelena/Shutterstock.com; p.114 © LittleCuckoo/Shutterstock.com; p.115 © Aliaksandr Radzko/Shutterstock.com; p.116 © Sudowoodo/Shutterstock.com; pp.116-117 – origami instructions © tofang/Shutterstock.com; p.118 © M-vector/Shutterstock.com; pp.118-119 – Hamish Braid; p.120 © Hamish braid; p.121 © LynxVector/Shutterstock.com; p.122 © David Smart/Tamara Kulikova/Shutterstock.com; p.123 © Juli92/Shutterstock.com; p.124 © Wiktoria Matynia/Shutterstock.com; p.125 © bounward/Shutterstock.com; p.126 © Kaissa/Shutterstock.com; p.127 © Classica2/Shutterstock.com; p.128 © StockSmartStart/Shutterstock.com; p.129 © VILOGSIGN/Shutterstock.com; p.130 © Alexander Ryabintsev/Shutterstock.com; p.131 © Agnes Kantaruk/Shutterstock.com; p.132 © Francois Poirier/Shutterstock.com; p.132-33 © Alhovik/Shutterstock.com; p.134 © i3alda/Shutterstock.com; p.135 © Strejman/Shutterstock.com; p.136 © Wiktoria Matynia/Shutterstock.com; p.137 © notbad/Shutterstock.com; p.138 © NatBasil/Shutterstock.com; p.138 – top image © Natalia Pushchina; bottom image © Warren Millar/Shutterstock.com; p.139 – top image © Uber Images; middle image © Roman Samborskyi; bottom image © HBRH/Shutterstock.com; p.140 © designmaestro/Shutterstock.com; p.141 © matius/Shutterstock.com; p.142 – cocktail © Macrovector; mint © Mariya II/Shutterstock.com; icon © Rauf Aliyev/Shutterstock.com; p.143 – cocktail © Macrovector; mango © Victoria Sergeeva/Shutterstock.com; p.144 © veronchick84/Shutterstock.com; p.145 © Bobnevv/Shutterstock.com; p.146 © PPVector/Shutterstock.com; p.147 © A_KUDR/Shutterstock.com; p.148 © puruan/Shutterstock.com; p.149 © ProStockStudio/Shutterstock.com; p.150 © vectorchef/Shutterstock.com; p.151 © bounward/Shutterstock.com; p.152 © DEmax/Shutterstock.com; p.154 © Creative icon styles/Shutterstock.com; p.155 © David Petrik/Shutterstock.com; p.156 © bounward/Shutterstock.com; p.157 © Jozsef Bagota/Shutterstock.com; p.160 © bounward/Shutterstock.com

Have you enjoyed this book?
If you're interested in finding out more about our books, find us on online at
skyhorsepublishing.com